Thank you Grampa for helping with my book

Second Printing, 2016

ISBN 978-0-9867593-4-5

A love hug is a hug that you give to someone you love.

You can give a love hug to a person or an animal.

Sometimes it can be a really big hug.

Sometimes it can be a little hug. It doesn't matter how big it is as long as you love them.

You can give love hugs at home.

You can give love hugs at school.

You can give love hugs at Nana's house.

You can give a love hug anywhere.

You give a love hug to Daddy when it's time to go to bed.

You can give a love hug to mommy when she gives you a bandage.

You can give a love hug when you say good-bye.

You can give a love hug when you are happy to see someone.

You can give someone a love hug when they give a hug to you.

You can give someone a hug just to give them a hug.

You can give a love hug to make someone happy.

You can give a love hug just to say 'I love you'

CPSIA information can be obtained
at www.ICGtesting.com
Printed in the USA
LVOW05s0339160616

492793LV00024B/121/P